CONTENTS

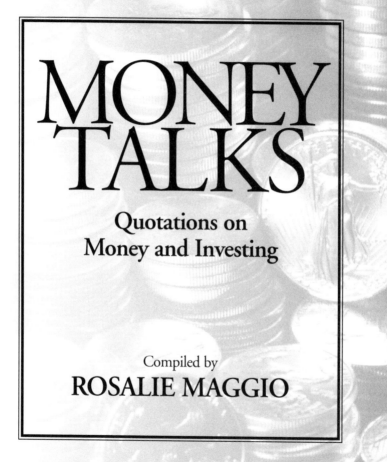

MONEY TALKS

Quotations on Money and Investing

Compiled by
ROSALIE MAGGIO

PRENTICE HALL PRESS

When money talks,
there are few interruptions.

HERBERT V. PROCHNOW

To Paul J. Maggio
loved and loving father
exemplary man
and astute investor

INTRODUCTION

Think of this collection of quotations on money and investments as a rather chatty, bookish, and occasionally witty financial adviser. In it, you'll find ruminations on money, guidelines for investing, and conflicting advice. Yes, conflicting advice. On the advice of counsel, I have included opposing opinions so that should you invest—and lose—everything you own on the basis of quotations found here, and thus feel very litigious toward me, I can point to another quotation and say, "Ah, but we also say that!" No, actually, the advice is conflicting because even today, as advanced technologically as we are, not everyone agrees on the best strategies for making, saving, and investing money.

Money is a mystery. Not only is our behavior with respect to money sometimes puzzling and erratic, but our feelings about money are often contradictory, illogical, deep-rooted, and scarcely known even to our most secret selves. We are getting better at handling money, but what it means to us, how we use it to express ourselves, and how it can help us become all that we are meant to be remain murky issues.

Money is a blessing. As a nation we have come of age with the expression "filthy lucre" buried in our psyches. We at once adore and disdain money, respect unduly those who have it and castigate them with stereotyped labels and assumptions. Intellectually, we know that money in itself is neither good nor bad. Emotionally, we are not so sure. Many people make and spend money in ways that beautify and enhance our world. Many have made an art of sharing what they have, of using their money like yeast to grow great loaves of benefits where there were none before. In the process, they find themselves enriched tenfold, although the coin may be recognizable only to them.

Money is a response. We use it to express our social values, our gratitude, our appreciation, our pleasure, our support. Money gives us the ability to respond (response-ability), and its empowering use often defines the truly responsible among us.

Money is always on its way somewhere. What we do with it while it's in our keeping will say much about us—as will the direction it takes after we speed it on its way. This little "financial adviser" will bring you hours of thought-provoking, useful, and memorable quotations on money and investing—but only you can put a personal spin on the ideas and use them to bless yourself, your loved ones, your community, and the global village.

MONEY

Today money is a favorite topic of conversation in many settings. The financial page of the daily newspaper is read about as avidly as the sports page or the comics. There has probably never been a cocktail party at which the subject of taxes, the cost of living, or the price of real estate has not been discussed. In gossip circles, who did what with whom is rivaled only by who paid how much for what.

HERB GOLDBERG AND
ROBERT T. LEWIS

1

In its essential form, money is simply a commodity which is so generally desirable that it is acceptable to virtually anyone in an intermediate exchange. It is no less a commodity than pickled herring, but it has a longer shelf life (durability), has a universally recognized value, is divisible, and is portable.

VICTOR SPERANDEO

Money has created a unified world economy that includes the price of milk and eggs in the market at Bandiagara as well as the price of stock in Sara Lee Foods or PepsiCo on the New York Stock Exchange. Although fluctuations in politics, religion, technology, and even the weather can play a role in any of these endeavors, money constitutes the basis of the entire system and forms the crucial link in establishing value, facilitating exchange, and creating commerce. Money unites them all together into a single global system. It is the tie that binds us all.

JACK WEATHERFORD

Money ranks as one of the primary materials with which mankind builds the architecture of civilization.

LEWIS H. LAPHAM

Money is one of the most fundamental of all Man's inventions. Every branch of knowledge has its fundamental discovery. In mechanics it is the wheel, in science fire, in politics the vote. Similarly, in economics, in the whole commercial side of Man's social existence, money is the essential invention on which all the rest is based.

GEOFFREY CROWTHER

People keep telling us about their love affairs, when what we really want to know is how much money they make and how they manage on it.

MIGNON MCLAUGHLIN

Money is like fire, an element as little troubled by moralizing as earth, air and water. Men can employ it as a tool or they can dance around it as if it were the incarnation of a god. Money votes socialist or monarchist, finds a profit in pornography or translations from the Bible, commissions Rembrandt and underwrites the technology of Auschwitz. It acquires its meaning from the uses to which it is put.

LEWIS H. LAPHAM

Money, which represents the prose of life, and which is hardly spoken of in parlors without an apology, is, in its effects and laws, as beautiful as roses.

RALPH WALDO EMERSON

Money is power, freedom, a cushion, the root of all evil, the sum of blessings.

CARL SANDBURG

Why doesn't someone write a poem on money? Nobody does anything but abuse it. There's hardly a good word for money to be found in literature. The poets and writers have been needy devils and thought to brave out their beggary by pretending to despise it. This shows what liars poets and literary men are. The chief cry of their hearts has never found its way into their books during the last three thousand years.

JOHN JAY CHAPMAN

I'm tired of Love: I'm still more tired of Rhyme. But Money gives me pleasure all the time.

HILLAIRE BELLOC

The complex mechanisms of the modern world depend as certainly on the faith in money as the structures of the medieval world depended upon faith in God.

LEWIS H. LAPHAM

Money constitutes the focal point of modern world culture. Money defines relationships among people, not just between customer and merchant in the marketplace or employer and laborer in the workplace. Increasingly in modern society, money defines relationships between parent and child, among friends, between politicians and constituents, among neighbors, and between clergy and parishioners.

JACK WEATHERFORD

Money talks. The more money, the louder it talks.

ARNOLD ROTHSTEIN

Money speaks sense in a language all nations understand.

APHRA BEHN

Money not only speaks sense, it also imposes that sense on whatever society it conquers, and it does so in a way that subjugates all other institutions and systems. From virtually the moment of its invention, money became ever more important in Western society and eventually overwhelmed the feudal system and the aristocratic hierarchies of earlier civilizations.

JACK WEATHERFORD

When money talks, there are few interruptions.

HERBERT V. PROCHNOW

That money talks
I'll not deny.
I heard it once:
It said, "Goodbye."

RICHARD ARMOUR

7

When a fellow says it ain't the money but the principle of the thing, it's the money.

KIN HUBBARD

There are only three things you can do with a dollar: spend, loan, or own.

VENITA VANCASPEL

Money is like a flower. If you squeeze it, you will crush the life out of it.

VENITA VANCASPEL

I finally know what distinguishes man from the other beasts: financial worries.

JULES RENARD

It is very funny about money. The thing that differentiates man from animals is money. All animals have the same emotions and the same ways as men. Anybody who has lots of animals around knows that. But the thing no animal can do is count, and the thing no animal can know is money.

GERTRUDE STEIN

When money stands still, it is no longer money.

GEORG SIMMEL

Money is nearly always related to action.

MICHAEL PHILLIPS

Money only really shows itself when it is in motion.

ANTHONY SAMPSON

Money is only useful when you get rid of it. It is like the odd card in "Old Maid"; the player who is finally left with it has lost.

EVELYN WAUGH

Money, n. A blessing that is of no advantage to us excepting when we part with it.

AMBROSE BIERCE

Do you realize what a rare and beautiful thing cash is? There are people making $200,000, $300,000, $400,000 a year who haven't seen $1,000 in cash in the past twenty years. It's all plastic, checks and numbers in bank statements. It's never crisp, crunchy, crackly, comely, curvaceous, cold, hard cash.

HARVEY MACKAY

It is not so good *with* money as it is bad *without* it.

YIDDISH PROVERB

Money helps, though not so much as you think when you don't have it.

LOUISE ERDRICH

Money is better than poverty, if only for financial reasons.

WOODY ALLEN

Money isn't everything, but lack of money isn't anything.

FRANKLIN P. ADAMS

They say money isn't everything. That's true—but look how many things it is.

ROBERT ORBEN

Money isn't everything, your health is the other ten percent.

LILLIAN DAY

In America, money takes the place of God.

ANZIA YEZIERSKA

This is a speculating and selfish age; and to think "money will answer all things" is too much the characteristic of Americans.

SARAH J. HALE

In our society, money is everything. For Americans, it is how we keep score.

KATHLEEN GURNEY

It is part of the ethos of this country that you *ought* to be rich. You ought to be, unless you have taken some specific vow of poverty such as the priesthood, scholarship, teaching, or civil service, because money is the way we keep score.

"ADAM SMITH"

The amount of money we have establishes how our fellow members of society view our success. "If you are so smart, why ain't you rich?"

HENRY CLASING

Money . . . brings out the best and the worst in people.

HERB GOLDBERG AND
ROBERT T. LEWIS

A man's treatment of money is the most decisive test of his character—how he makes it and how he spends it.

JAMES MOFFATT

Money had taken over many attributes of a religion. Like a religion it binds together different parts of the world, providing the means by which people and nations judge each other. Like a religion it demands great faith, a huge priesthood with rituals and incantations that few ordinary people understand. Like missionaries, the bankers and brokers travel the still unconverted parts of the world, bringing the deserts and jungles into the same system of values, seeking to convert still more tribes to their own faith in credit, interest rates, and the sacred bottom line. Today it is bank managers rather than priests who are the guardians of people's secrets and confessionals.

ANTHONY SAMPSON

I have nothing but contempt for the people who despise money. They are hypocrites or fools. Money is like a sixth sense without which you cannot make a complete use of the other five. Without an adequate income half the possibilities of life are shut off.

W. SOMERSET MAUGHAM

Money may be the husk of many things, but not the kernel. It brings you food, but not appetite; medicine, but not health; acquaintances, but not friends; servants, but not faithfulness; days of joy, but not peace or happiness.

HENRIK IBSEN

Money, to some extent, sometimes lets you be in more interesting environments. But it can't change how many people love you or how healthy you are.

WARREN BUFFETT

Money, after all, is extremely simple. It is a part of our transportation system. It is a simple and direct method of conveying goods from one person to another. Money is in itself most admirable. It is essential. It is not intrinsically evil. It is one of the most useful devices in social life. And when it does what it was intended to do, it is all help and no hindrance.

HENRY FORD

The only problems money can solve are money problems.

JAY W. FORRESTER

Money is a central issue. The money you earn is the physical representation of the life energy you have expended to earn it.

SAMUEL CASE

Money is the last enemy that shall never be subdued. While there is flesh there is money—or the want of money; but money is always on the brain so long as there is a brain in reasonable order.

SAMUEL BUTLER

The world stands on three things: money, money, and money.

YIDDISH PROVERB

Those who never think of money need a great deal of it.

AGATHA CHRISTIE

Anyone pretending he has no interest in money is either a fool or a knave.

LESLIE FORD

A fool and his money are soon parted.

ANONYMOUS

Mark's Law of Monetary Equalization: A fool and your money are soon partners.

ARTHUR BLOCH

There was a time when a fool and his money were soon parted, but now it happens to everybody.

ADLAI STEVENSON

A fool and his money are soon parted. What I want to know is how they got together in the first place.

CYRIL FLETCHER

Creatively pursued, the money game is indeed the most exciting game of all.

PAULA NELSON

The only way not to think about money is to have a great deal of it.

EDITH WHARTON

There is nothing so habit-forming as money.

DON MARQUIS

I don't like money, actually, but it quiets my nerves.

JOE LOUIS

Money is shy and elusive. It must be wooed and won by methods not unlike those used by a determined lover. . . . Riches are shy and timid. They have to be "attracted."

NAPOLEON HILL

Money is a living entity, and it responds to energy exactly the same way you do. It is drawn to those who welcome it, those who respect it. Wouldn't you rather be with people who respect you and who don't want you to be something you're not? Your money feels the same way.

SUZE ORMAN

I've noticed that people who don't respect money don't have any.

PAUL GETTY

To me, money is alive. It is almost human. If you treat it with real sympathy and kindness and consideration, it will be a good servant and work hard for you, and stay with you and take care of you. If you treat it arrogantly and contemptuously, as if it were not human, as if it were only a slave and could work without limit, it will turn on you with a great revenge and leave you to look after yourself alone.

KATHARINE BUTLER HATHAWAY

I have come to think that money is very much like a person, and it will respond when you treat it as you would a cherished friend—never fearing it, pushing it away, pretending it doesn't exist, or turning away from its needs, never clutching it so hard that it hurts . . . if you tend it like the living entity it is, then it will flourish, grow, take care of you for as long as you need it.

SUZE ORMAN

21

Money's queer. It goes where it's wanted.

AGATHA CHRISTIE

Money, it turned out, was exactly like sex, you thought of nothing else if you didn't have it and thought of other things if you did.

JAMES BALDWIN

Money may not be your best friend, but it's the quickest to act, and seems to be favorably recognized in more places than most friends are.

MYRTLE REED

People who think money can do anything may very well be suspected of doing anything for money.

MARY PETTIBONE POOLE

Money changes people just as often as it changes hands.

AL BATT

The surest way to ruin a man who doesn't know how to handle money is to give him some.

GEORGE BERNARD SHAW

Money is very much a state of mind.

MICHAEL PHILLIPS

What's a thousand dollars? Mere chicken feed. A poultry matter.

GROUCHO MARX

MAKING IT

To learn the value of money, it is not necessary to know the nice things it can get for you, you
have to have experienced the trouble of getting it.

PHILIPPE HÉRIAT

Money is the seed of money, and the first
guinea is sometimes more difficult to acquire than
the second million.

JEAN JACQUES ROUSSEAU

The happiest time in any man's life is when he is in red-hot pursuit of a dollar with a reasonable prospect of overtaking it.

HENRY WHEELER SHAW

Starting out to make money is the greatest mistake in life. Do what you feel you have a flair for doing, and if you are good enough at it money will come.

WILLIAM ROOTES

Do what you love, the money will follow.

MARSHA SINETAR

Money will come when you are doing the right thing. . . . Worry about your ability to do it and your competence to do it but certainly do not worry about the money.

MICHAEL PHILLIPS

Find something you love to do and you'll never have to work a day in your life.

HARVEY MACKAY

Money is a by-product of something I like to do very much. Every day, when I get to the office, so to speak, I do a little tap dance.

WARREN BUFFETT

I believe the power to make money is a gift from God.

JOHN D. ROCKEFELLER

One must choose, in life, between making money and spending it. There's no time to do both.

EDOUARD BOURDET

The methods that help a man acquire a fortune are the very ones that keep him from enjoying it.

ANTOINE DE RIVAROL

Persistence is an essential factor in the procedure of transmuting desire into its monetary equivalent.

NAPOLEON HILL

The salary of the chief executive of the large corporation is not a market award for achievement. It is frequently in the nature of a warm personal gesture by the individual to himself.

JOHN KENNETH GALBRAITH

Every morning I get up and look through the Forbes list of the richest people in America. If I'm not there, I go to work.

ROBERT ORBEN

The safest way to double your money is to fold it over once and put it in your pocket.

KIN HUBBARD

It's easier to earn money than to keep it.

YIDDISH PROVERB

MANAGING IT

Some people seem to have a gift for managing money. They make good use of whatever funds they have, be they great or small. Other people are forever being pushed around or rendered unhappy by money problems of one sort or another. Is there any basic difference between the two types? I think there is. One regards money as a medium of exchange—nothing more. The other lets money become a symbol of something else.

SMILEY BLANTON

Of all the activities you must cram into your busy life, managing your money is the one you can least afford to overlook. . . . The biggest mistake you can make with money is neglect. You might as well leave your dollar bills outside in a high wind.

MARY L. SPROUSE

A faithfully kept program of savings and conservative investments can give you more money and a better life than that of your neighbors who spend everything they get. This is probably the oldest financial advice in the world, but there are some things you can't improve on.

JANE BRYANT QUINN

Managing money usually requires more skill than making it.

ROY L. SMITH

A person is more likely to be successful managing money if he uses spiritual principles, and the more you practice spirituality, the more you learn.

SIR JOHN TEMPLETON

Once you begin taking care of your money, I can promise that your money in turn will take care of you.

SUZE ORMAN

It has been said that if you aim at nothing in life, you are likely to hit nothing! I have never had anyone come to me and say, "Venita, I plan to fail." Yet I have observed many who failed to plan and who unfortunately met with the same dismal results.

VENITA VANCASPEL

Three reasons not to have a plan: 1. You're rich enough to buy anything you want and still have plenty of money left over. 2. I forget the other two.

JANE BRYANT QUINN

SAVING IT

In the long run, it's not just how much money you make that will determine your future prosperity. It's how much of that money you put to work by saving it and investing it.

PETER LYNCH

You're worth what you saved, not the millions you made.

JOHN BOYLE O'REILLY

The road to poverty is paved with the good intentions of those who wanted to save but never got around to it.

WILLIAM NICKERSON

If you saved money in the old days you were considered a miser; nowadays, you're a wonder.

JOEY ADAMS

It seems like only yesterday that savers were dorks. They kept piggy banks. They drove last year's cars. They fished in their change purses for nickels while the superstars flashed credit cards. Today, values have changed. The new object of veneration is not money on the hoof but money in the bank—and the dorks all have it.

JANE BRYANT QUINN

Saving is a very fine thing. Especially when your parents have done it for you.

WINSTON CHURCHILL

Money that may never be spent is nothing but a miser's toy. Saving as an exercise in self-denial is an invalid goal, a sick use of money.

CATHERINE CROOK DE CAMP

Savings will not make you rich. Only canny investments do that. The role of savings is to keep you from becoming poor.

JANE BRYANT QUINN

Bank accounts are like toothpaste: easy to take out but hard to put back.

ROBERT ACKERSTROM

The shortest recorded period of time lies between the minute you put some money away for a rainy day and the unexpected arrival of rain.

JANE BRYANT QUINN

SPENDING IT

The self that saves feels himself thwarted at every turn by the self that spends, and the self that spends is irritated by the knowledge that the self that saves is constantly watching him and grudging him every penny in his fingers.

ROBERT LYND

Living on a budget is the same as living beyond your means, except that you have a record of it.

ANONYMOUS

The individual serves the industrial system not by supplying it with savings and the resulting capital; he serves it by consuming its products.

JOHN KENNETH GALBRAITH

In the comparatively short time between my childhood and my daughter's, the business society has ceased urging people to produce and is now exerting its very considerable influence to get them to consume.

MARGARET HALSEY

Consumerism is our national religion.

JENNIFER STONE

Democracy always makes for materialism, because the only kind of equality that you can guarantee to a whole people is, broadly speaking, physical.

KATHARINE FULLERTON GEROULD

The metabolism of a consumer society requires it continually to eat and excrete, every day throwing itself away in plastic bags.

SHANA ALEXANDER

It's easy to meet expenses—everywhere we go, there they are.

ANONYMOUS

The pyramids were built for pharaohs on the happy theory that they could take their stuff with them. Versailles was built for kings on the theory that they should live surrounded by the finest stuff. The Mall of America is built on the premise that we should all be able to afford this stuff. It may be a shallow culture, but it's by-God democratic. Sneer if you dare; this is something new in world history.

MOLLY IVINS

Oh money, money, money
I'm not necessarily one of those who thinks
 thee holy,
But I often stop to wonder
How thou canst go out so fast when thou
 comest in so slowly.

OGDEN NASH

It does seem to be true that the more you get the more you spend. It is rather like being on a golden treadmill.

CHARLES ALLSOP

Never ask of money spent
Where the spender thinks it went.
Nobody was ever meant
To remember or invent
What he did with every cent.

ROBERT FROST

He who buys what he does not want ends in wanting what he cannot buy.

MRS. ALEC-TWEEDIE

41

SHARING IT

Whoever perpetrated the mathematical inaccuracy "Two can live as cheaply as one" has a lot to answer for.

CAREN MEYER

Surplus wealth is a sacred trust which its possessor is bound to administer in his lifetime for the good of the community.

ANDREW CARNEGIE

While everyone knows what money *can't* buy, there are obviously things that money *can* buy: a sense of security, a comfortable retirement, and an ability to provide for your family. Even from a religious standpoint, money doesn't have to be such a bad thing. In fact, if it's used to help others, money can be a very positive force.

JOEL GREENBLATT

It is an ignorant, or a very sordid world where people are poor because there is too much; and yet this is true today. Sometime, perhaps, our captains of industry who have already solved the problem of production will take up the problem of distribution.

CLARENCE DARROW

It is hard to interest those who have everything in those who have nothing.

HELEN KELLER

The old thought that one cannot be rich except at the expense of his neighbor, must pass away. True prosperity adds to the richness of the whole world, such as that of the man who makes two trees grow where only one grew before. The parasitical belief in prosperity as coming by the sacrifices of others has no place in the mind that thinks true. "My benefit is your benefit, your success is my success," should be the basis of all our wealth.

ANNE RIX MILTZ

There are two things needed in these days: first, for rich men to find out how poor men live; and second, for poor men to know how rich men work.

E. ATKINSON

Wealth is only a source of happiness when it is used to do good for others.

DENIS WAITLEY AND RENI L. WITT

I make money using my brains and lose money listening to my heart. But in the long run my books balance pretty well.

KATE SEREDY

Capitalism begins with giving. Not from greed, avarice or even self-love can one expect the rewards of commerce, but from a spirit closely akin to altruism, a regard for the needs of others, a benevolent, outgoing, and courageous temper of mind.

GEORGE GILDER

The results of philanthropy are always beyond calculation.

MIRIAM BEARD

To despise riches may indeed, be philosophic, but to dispense them worthily must surely be more beneficial to mankind.

FANNY BURNEY

Being moderate with oneself and generous with others; this is what is meant by having a just relationship with money, by being free as far as money is concerned.

NATALIA GINZBURG

Money-giving is a good criterion of a person's mental health. Generous people are rarely mentally ill people.

KARL MENNINGER

I have tried to teach people that there are three kicks in every dollar: one, when you make it—and how I love to make a dollar; two, when you have it—and I have the Yankee lust for saving. The third kick is when you give it away—and it is the biggest kick of all.

WILLIAM ALLEN WHITE

INVESTING IT

Put not your trust in money, but put your money in trust.

OLIVER WENDELL HOLMES, SR.

There is a secret to investing that cuts a path directly to the profits that you're looking for. The secret is simplicity. The more elementary your investment style, the more confident you can be of making money in the long run.

JANE BRYANT QUINN

The true secret of success in the investment and speculative world is not so much which good securities to buy, but rather which investments to avoid.

MORTON SHULMAN

To achieve *satisfactory* investment results is easier than most people realize; to achieve *superior* results is harder than it looks.

BENJAMIN GRAHAM

People who consistently make money in their investments succeed because of their *understanding*—more than because of information. They apply basic principles of the real world to their investments, rather than allowing specific information to direct them.

HARRY BROWNE

Investment is a game, and calls for the same qualities required to win at any game: You have to love the game and have an intense desire to win. Whatever strategy you follow, you should follow three rules: Be thorough, tough-minded, and flexible; know a great deal about any company you buy into; and only buy when the company is misunderstood by the market.

JOHN TRAIN

To invest successfully over a lifetime does not require a stratospheric IQ, unusual business insights, or inside information. What's needed is a sound intellectual framework for making decisions and the ability to keep emotions from corroding that framework.

WARREN BUFFETT

I suspect that temperament costs investors more than ignorance.

JOHN TRAIN

Investors operate with limited funds and limited intelligence: They do not need to know everything. As long as they understand something better than others, they have an edge.

GEORGE SOROS

Most new investors try various markets, lose money, and finally acquire some knowledge through bitter experience. This is roughly analogous to learning how to drive by having a series of accidents.

SAMUEL CASE

Quinn's First Law of Investing is never to buy anything whose price you can't follow in the newspapers. An investment without a public market-place attracts the fabulists the way picnics attract ants. Stockbrokers and financial planners can tell you anything they want, because no one really knows what's true. The First Corollary to Quinn's First Law states that, even when the price is in the newspa-pers, you shouldn't buy anything too complex to explain to the average 12-year-old.

JANE BRYANT QUINN

We may not know when we're well off, but investment salesmen get on to it somehow.

KIN HUBBARD

The world is not transformed from one day to the next, and the average investor makes less money with his brain than what in chess is called his *Sitzfleisch*, or patient rear end.

JOHN TRAIN

It never is your thinking that makes big money, it's the sitting.

JESSE LIVERMORE

I'm not convinced, yet, that simple passive investing isn't the best way to go for the vast bulk of all investors.

MERTON MILLER

In real estate, they speak of location, location, location. The investment equivalent is persistence, persistence, persistence.

PETER J. TANOUS

Good investment practices can almost be called studies in good character . . . The greatest investors are often outstanding human beings, insofar as they exemplify the highest achievement in one or more human characteristics like patience, diligence, perceptiveness, and common sense. Because remember: Dealing in money, the investor constantly must avoid his own *instinctive temptation* toward fear and greed. Fear and greed will ruin your investment returns.

DAVID AND TOM GARDNER

Avoid greed and fear. These are the investor's Achilles heels. Keeping all your money in the bank earning 3% interest is just as foolish as dumping your entire savings into the market thinking you'll make a quick buck.

NANCY DUNNAN

The ability to make a decision is another characteristic of a winner in money matters. I have found over and over again that those who succeed in making large sums of money reach decisions very promptly and change them, if at all, very slowly. I have also found that people who fail to make money reach decisions very slowly, if at all, and change them frequently and quickly.

VENITA VANCASPEL

The individual who acts and dares to make a decision now—not tomorrow—is the one who ends up with the millions.

MARK OLIVER HAROLDSEN

The man who insists upon seeing with perfect clearness before he decides, never decides.

HENRI FRÉDÉRIC AMIEL

If you have never missed when investing, you haven't been in there trying.

VENITA VANCASPEL

If you don't profit from your investment mistakes, someone else will.

YALE HIRSCH

Nobody has ever bet enough on the winning horse.

ANONYMOUS

The gambling known as business looks with austere disfavor upon the business known as gambling.

AMBROSE BIERCE

If you bet on a horse, that's gambling. If you bet you can make three spades, that's entertainment. If you bet cotton will go up three points, that's business. See the difference?

BLACKIE SHERRODE

All investments are unforgiving of human error. There are no exceptions.

HARVEY MACKAY

Invest in haste, repent in leisure.

CHRISTOPHER WEBER AND LEONARD REISS

In the investment game risk and returns are inseparable.

DONALD R. KURTZ

The higher the yield, the higher the risk. A high yield is designed to attract investors. An outrageously high yield attracts fools.

NANCY DUNNAN

A few investments are in fact so safe that they cost you money.

MARY ELIZABETH SCHLAYER
AND MARILYN H. COOLEY

The bad investments pretend to be all things to all people. "Buy me," they whisper, "and you'll get your three wishes—no risk, high income, and high growth." Some throw in a fourth wish, tax deferral, just for spice. But no single investment can make all your wishes come true. . . . When you go for high income, you give up some safety and growth. When you go for high growth, you give up some safety and income. When you go for safety, you lose growth and income. You have to decide which matters most. Any investment that promises all three is leading you down the garden path.

JANE BRYANT QUINN

In investing money, the amount of interest you want should depend on whether you want to eat well or sleep well.

J. KENFIELD MORLEY

Conservative investors sleep well.

PHILIP A. FISHER

Usually the way we miss opportunities in this business is by saying, "It looks too good to be true," and then not doing anything. Too often we think that everybody else must know something that we don't, and I think that's a critical mistake. How many times have you heard someone put down an idea you're excited about by saying, "If it's such a good idea, why isn't everyone doing it?" This is the battle cry of mediocrity. Think about it for a minute. Any investment opportunity that everyone else is doing is by definition a bad idea. I would always recommend doing the opposite.

MARK RITCHIE

To obtain better than average investment results over a long pull requires a policy of selection or operation possessing a twofold merit: (1) It must meet objective or rational tests of underlying soundness; and (2) it must be different from the policy followed by most investors or speculators.

BENJAMIN GRAHAM

Much has been written in the literature of investments on the importance of contrary opinion. Contrary opinion, however, is not enough. I have seen investment people so imbued with the need to go contrary to the general trend of thought that they completely overlook the corollary of all this which is: when you do go contrary to the general trend of investment thinking, you must be very, very sure that you are right.

PHILIP A. FISHER

The investor who permits himself to be stampeded or unduly worried by unjustified market declines in his holdings is perversely transforming his basic advantage into a basic disadvantage. That man would be better off if his stocks had no market quotation at all, for he would then be spared the mental anguish caused him by *other persons'* mistakes of judgment.

BENJAMIN GRAHAM

In all games the difference between the amateur and the professional is that the professional plays the odds, while the amateur, whether he realizes it or not, is among other things a thrill seeker. Investment, too, is part a science and part a game, and just as in poker, you need to sort out your motives.

JOHN TRAIN

Investing without research is like playing stud poker and never looking at the cards.

PETER LYNCH

Don't be overly impressed with investment firms that have had highly successful investment performance records within the recent past. You might be giving money to an organization that is so happily riding the last trend that they will be the last to admit when the trend is ending.

BENNETT W. GOODSPEED

To the list of famous oxymorons—military intelligence, learned professor, deafening silence, and jumbo shrimp—I'd add professional investing.

PETER LYNCH

In all my investment strategies, I bet more on the jockeys than on the horses—the folks managing the investments more than the investments themselves.

LOU DOBBS

Investment opportunities change over the long term. You want a pilot who can fly even if the weather changes.

SHELBY WHITE

You should invest in a business that even a fool can run, because someday a fool will.

WARREN BUFFETT

Our conclusion is that, with few exceptions, when management with a reputation for brilliance tackles a business with a reputation for poor fundamental economics, it is the reputation of the business that remains intact.

WARREN BUFFETT

You can't be sentimental about your investments and make money from them.

TYLER G. HICKS

Investment is most intelligent when it is most *businesslike*. It is amazing to see how many capable businessmen try to operate in Wall Street with complete disregard of all the sound principles through which they have gained success in their own undertakings.

BENJAMIN GRAHAM

In many ways, large profits are even more insidious than large losses in terms of emotional destabilization. I think it's important not to be emotionally attached to large profits. I've certainly made some of my worst trades after long periods of winning. When you're on a big winning streak, there's a temptation to think you're doing something special, which will allow you to continue to propel yourself upward. You start to think that you can afford to make shoddy decisions. You can imagine what happens next. As a general rule, losses make you strong and profits make you weak.

WILLIAM ECKHARDT

The mutual fund is a wonderful invention for people who have neither the time nor the inclination to test their wits against the stock market, as well as for people with small amounts of money to invest who seek diversification.

PETER LYNCH

65

For several years I tracked the performance of the family's socially screened investments against the performance of the traditional investments. To my surprise, and to the surprise of some professional money managers with whom I worked, the social investments, as a whole, outperformed the traditional investments in total return.... Socially responsible investing ... and socially responsible business practices can pay off very handsomely relative to investments and business conduct done solely "for profit" and ... social investments and socially responsible companies can weather difficult economic times better than their "profit only" counterparts.

RITCHIE P. LOWRY

A mutual fund can do for you what you would do for yourself if you had sufficient time, training, and money to diversify, plus the temperament to stand back from your money and make rational decisions.

VENITA VANCASPEL

Mutual Funds are rarely bought at an investor's whim. The management has hard-working and persuasive salesmen out, digging into new territory all over, not just in the stock-conscious coastal areas and big cities. They call on people and explain the advantages of their wares, and answer questions. They call again if they are given any encouragement; they call again if they are not given any encouragement.

FRED SCHWED, JR.

If an investor ... makes choices using asset class portfolios, life suddenly gets real simple. He doesn't have to burn the midnight oil figuring out what stocks to buy or what fund to buy. He doesn't have to buy all of those reports that list mutual funds; he doesn't have to read publications or listen to programs that are void of substantial content. I like to refer to this as "investment pornography."

REX SINQUEFIELD

Diversification is a protection against ignorance. [It] makes very little sense for those who know what they're doing.

WARREN BUFFETT

Gentlemen prefer bonds.

ANDREW MELLON

Gentlemen who prefer bonds don't know what they're missing.

PETER LYNCH

Never try to time the bond market. Anyone who claims to know the future of interest rates is certifiable.

JANE BRYANT QUINN

I think the key to our success, our long-term record picking out the fallen angels in bonds and convertible preferred, is that we are buying yield-to-maturity for very long periods of time. So our turnover is very low. We ride through overreactions in those issues. By and large, we're buyers when there are panic sellers out there.

ERIC RYBACK

Options carry a particularly high degree of risk. Investing in this area without a good understanding of how options work is like running through a dynamite factory with a burning match—you may live, but you're still an idiot.

JOEL GREENBLATT

You don't date an annuity, you marry it.
An annuity isn't a mutual fund that you buy today
and sell tomorrow. Nor is it a certificate of deposit,
ready for any new use at maturity. When you buy an
annuity, you are making (or ought to be making) a
15- or 20-year commitment, at least.

JANE BRYANT QUINN

Hedge funds remind me of the Groucho
Marx line about clubs. The ones that will take your
money may not be the ones you want to invest with.

SHELBY WHITE

THE STOCK MARKET

If a graduating MBA were to ask me, "How do I get rich in a hurry?" I would not respond with quotations from Ben Franklin or Horatio Alger, but would instead hold my nose with one hand and point with the other toward Wall Street.

WARREN BUFFETT

In the course of evolution and a higher civilization we might be able to get along comfortably without Congress, but without Wall Street never.

HENRY CLEWS

If Wall Street didn't exist, it would be necessary to invent it.

LOUIS ENGEL

The stock market is like some huge, enigmatic creature under continuous, intense scrutiny.

RICHARD SAUL WURMAN, ALAN SIEGEL,
KENNETH M. MORRIS

In spite of crashes, depressions, wars, recessions, ten different presidential administrations, and numerous changes in skirt lengths, stocks in general have paid off fifteen times as well as corporate bonds, and well over thirty times better than Treasury bills!

PETER LYNCH

Few human activities have been so exhaustively studied during the past fifty years, from so many angles and by so many different sorts of people, as has the buying and selling of corporate securities. The rewards which the stock market holds out to those who read it right are enormous; the penalties it exacts from careless, dozing or "unlucky" investors are calamitous—no wonder it has attracted some of the world's most astute accountants, analysts and researchers, along with a motley crew of eccentrics, mystics and "hunch players," and a multitude of just ordinary hopeful citizens.

JOHN MAGEE AND ROBERT D. EDWARDS

No matter what the stock market does, people want to know how it did it, why it did it, and why it didn't do something else.

RICHARD SAUL WURMAN, ALAN SIEGEL,
KENNETH M. MORRIS

No other investment rivals common stocks as a way of accumulating wealth. Unless you're flat broke, reading this from your death bed, and have no heirs, there will be a time in your life when it will make sense to hold common stocks.

MICHAEL O'HIGGINS

No one knows what stocks will do tomorrow, but the evidence is clear as to how they'll perform over 10 or 20 years. They will almost certainly go up. A lot.

JANE BRYANT QUINN

Anytime *is a good time to invest in the stock market*. . . . Whether the stock market is breaking new records or laying an egg, *today is still the best time to invest.*

JIM JORGENSEN

While it can't be said that life is always fair, in most cases and over the long term the stock market is. Despite being a card-carrying contrarian, I agree with the now widely accepted wisdom that for most people stocks are the investment vehicle of choice. As long as the economy and the individual businesses that make it up continue to grow, sooner or later the stock market will reflect this reality.

JOEL GREENBLATT

The thing that most affects the stock market is everything.

JAMES PLAYSTED WOOD

The stock market is an index of how investors feel about the future, not the present. In other words, it is a barometer, not a thermometer.

JOHN TRAIN

You have to be smart to succeed at this business. That shouldn't be surprising, but to many, it is. I suppose it's because so many people look at the stock market like a big casino where some lucky gamblers win. Not true.

PETER J. TANOUS

If you are ready to give up everything else—to study the whole history and background of the market and all the principal companies whose stocks are on the board as carefully as a medical student studies anatomy—if you can do all that, and, in addition, you have the cool nerves of a great gambler, the sixth sense of a clairvoyant, and the courage of a lion, you have a ghost of a chance.

BERNARD BARUCH

I'm constantly amazed at popular explanations of why stocks behave the way they do. . . . We've made great advances in eliminating ignorance and superstition in medicine and in weather reports, we laugh at our ancestors for blaming bad harvests on corn gods, and we wonder, "How could a smart man like Pythagoras think that evil spirits hide in rumpled bedsheets?" However, we're perfectly willing to believe that who wins the Super Bowl might have something to do with stock prices.

PETER LYNCH

There is no human activity that I know of to which people have a more irrational approach than the stock market.

NICOLAS DARVAS

Only a dreamer or a fool would pick a stock at random and expect it to take off like a space ship from its launching pad. Certainly this has happened—about as often as a dime-store clerk has become a Hollywood star or a boy born in a log cabin has been elected President of the United States—just often enough, that is, to keep alive the Great American Dream.

CATHERINE CROOK DE CAMP

It is personal preparation, as much as knowledge and research, that distinguishes the successful stockpicker from the chronic loser. Ultimately it is not the stock market nor even the companies themselves that determine an investor's fate. It is the investor.

PETER LYNCH

There are several different ways to make and keep money in Wall Street . . . one lucky break, or one supremely shrewd decision—can we tell them apart?—may count for more than a lifetime of journeyman efforts. But behind the luck, or the crucial decision, there must usually exist a background of preparation and disciplined capacity. One needs to be sufficiently established and recognized so that these opportunities will knock at his particular door. One must have the means, the judgment, and the courage to take advantage of them.

BENJAMIN GRAHAM

The secret to success in the markets lies not in discovering some incredible indicator or elaborate theory; rather, it lies within each individual.

JACK D. SCHWAGER

Everyone has the brainpower to make money in stocks. Not everyone has the stomach.

PETER LYNCH

Trading puts pressure on weaker human traits and seems to seek out each individual's Achilles' heel.

GIL BLAKE

The stock market demands conviction as surely as it victimizes the unconvinced.

PETER LYNCH

If you don't know who you are, the stock market is an expensive place to find out.

GEORGE GOODMAN

I can say that after years of studying traders, the best predictor of success is simply whether the person is improving with time and experience. Many traders unconsciously acknowledge their lack of progress by continually jumping from one system or methodology to another, never gaining true proficiency in any. As a result, these people end up with one year of experience six times instead of six years of experience.

CHARLES FAULKNER

If you want to make money in the stock market, *never be out of the stock market*.... The question isn't what do you think the stock market will do next, the question is what will you do next.

JIM JORGENSEN

It is my strong belief that one of the keys to building capital is preserving it during down periods in the market. This can be more important than outperforming the market on the upside.

WILLIAM J. LIPPMANN

History has shown the biggest risk is not being in the market when it drops, but being out of the market when it rises.

JIM JORGENSEN

Successful investing in the stock market is not brain surgery. Anyone can be a successful investor. The secret is no secret. It is simply that you confine your selections to blue chip stocks, you buy them when they are undervalued, and you sell them when they become overvalued.

GERALDINE WEISS AND GREGORY WEISS

Stocks are simple. All you do is buy shares in a great business for less than the business is intrinsically worth, with managers of the highest integrity and ability. Then you own those shares forever.

WARREN BUFFETT

Don't gamble; take all your savings and buy some good stock and hold it till it goes up, then sell it. If it don't go up, don't buy it.

WILL ROGERS

To pull off a great investment coup it is best to be the only substantial buyer of a stock in which you are building up a position. Napoleon observed that one good general was enough for an army, and the best generals of his time rarely held councils of war. Similarly, committee investing is almost always mediocre investing.

JOHN TRAIN

You should forget the short term, and not worry about the economy or the direction of the market. Instead, *buy a share of a company the way you buy a house: because you know all about it, and want to own it for a long time at that price.* In fact, you should only buy what you would be happy to own *in the absence of any market.*

JOHN TRAIN

The stock market seems to move according to the rules of gravity; you can fall 1,000 feet very quickly, but climbing 1,000 feet takes quite a bit more stamina.

RICHARD SAUL WURMAN, ALAN SIEGEL, KENNETH M. MORRIS

There is a way to make a lot of money in the market; unfortunately it is the same way to lose a lot of money in the market.

PETER PASSELL AND LEONARD ROSE

Last week is the time you should have either bought or sold, depending on which you didn't do.

LEONARD LOUIS LEVINSON

Well, the broker made money and the firm made money—and two out of three ain't bad.

ANONYMOUS

Let Wall Street have a nightmare and the whole country has to help get them back in bed again.

WILL ROGERS

Hot stocks can go up fast, usually out of sight of any of the known landmarks of value, but since there's nothing but hope and thin air to support them, they fall just as quickly. If you aren't clever at selling hot stocks (and the fact that you've bought them is a clue that you won't be), you'll soon see your profits turn into losses, because when the price falls, it's not going to fall slowly, nor is it likely to stop at the level where you jumped on.

PETER LYNCH

When a company president is ready to buy you lunch, it's time to sell the stock. When he has something really good, you can't get him on the phone.

PHIL STOLLER

When a corporation goes into the marketplace to buy back its own stock, it means management thinks the stock is undervalued. This is a smart time to buy.

NANCY DUNNAN

Getting the story on a company is a lot easier if you understand the basic business. That's why I'd rather invest in panty hose than in communications satellites, or in motel chains than in fiber optics. The simpler it is, the better I like it. When somebody says, "Any idiot could run this joint," that's a plus as far as I'm concerned, because sooner or later any idiot probably is going to be running it.

PETER LYNCH

Often there is no correlation between the success of a company's operations and the success of its stock over a few months or even a few years. In the long term, there is a 100 percent correlation between the success of the company and the success of its stock. This disparity is the key to making money; it pays to be patient, and to own successful companies.

PETER LYNCH

The big fortunes from single-company investments are almost always realized by persons who have a close relationship with the particular company—through employment, family connection, etc.—which justifies them in placing a large part of their resources in one medium and holding on to this commitment through all vicissitudes, despite numerous temptations to sell out at apparently high prices along the way.

BENJAMIN GRAHAM

The best stock to buy may be the one you already own.

PETER LYNCH

The business "grapevine" is a remarkable thing. It is amazing what an accurate picture of the relative points of strength and weakness of each company in an industry can be obtained from a representative cross-section of the opinions of those who in one way or another are concerned with any particular company.... Go to five companies in an industry, ask each of them intelligent questions about the points of strength and weakness of the other four, and nine times out of ten a surprisingly detailed and accurate picture of all five will emerge.

PHILIP A. FISHER

When bad things happen to good companies, it must be viewed as a buying opportunity rather than a bailout.

GERALDINE WEISS AND GREGORY WEISS

Great investment opportunities come around when excellent companies are surrounded by unusual circumstances that cause the stock to be misappraised.

WARREN BUFFETT

Historically, stocks are embraced as investments or dismissed as gambles in routine and circular fashion, and usually at the wrong times. Stocks are most likely to be accepted as prudent at the moment they're not.

PETER LYNCH

With companies of Dow stock caliber, there is more opportunity than risk. Bad news is usually good news because it makes strong stocks cheap.

MICHAEL O'HIGGINS

Never is there a better time to buy a stock than when a basically sound company, for whatever reason, temporarily falls out of favor with the investment community.

GERALDINE WEISS AND JANET LOWE

If you can't convince yourself "When I'm down 25 percent, I'm a buyer" and banish forever the fatal thought "When I'm down 25 percent, I'm a seller," then you'll never make a decent profit in stocks.

PETER LYNCH

If you have a tragic stock that has lost half of its value, and you can't find a better place to put the money, leave it there. In certain market periods, big losers that are still dependable companies own a higher probability for short-term gains than your typical momentum investor's darling.

DAVID AND TOM GARDNER

Most people get interested in stocks when everyone else is. The time to get interested is when no one else is. You can't buy what is popular and do well.

WARREN BUFFETT

MARKET LOSSES

The single most important reason that people lose money in the financial markets is that they don't cut their losses short. It is a curiosity of human nature that no matter how many books talk about this rule, and no matter how many experts offer this advice, people still keeping making the same mistake.

VICTOR SPERANDEO

Always leave a sinking ship. There's no virtue in hanging on to losers. And stocks don't have feelings.

NANCY DUNNAN

Take your losses quickly and your profits slowly. There is an old investment saying that the first loss in the market is the smallest loss. In my view, the way to make investment decisions is to take your losses quickly and your profits slowly. Yet most investors get emotionally confused and take their profits quickly and their losses slowly.

WILLIAM J. O'NEIL

When in doubt, get out!

VICTOR SPERANDEO

I don't think you can make money unless you're willing to lose it. Unless you have money that you can afford to lose and still sleep at night, you don't belong in the market. My willingness to lose is fundamental to my ability to make money in the markets.

MARK RITCHIE

There are few more certain ways of guaranteeing that you *will* lose than by trading money you can't afford to lose. If your trading capital is too important, you will be doomed to a number of fatal errors. You will miss out on some of the best trading opportunities because these are often the most risky. You will jump out of perfectly good positions prematurely on the first sign of adverse price movement only to then see the market go in the anticipated direction. You will be too quick to take the first bit of profit because of concern that the market will take it away from you.... In short, trading with "scared money" will lead to a host of negative emotions that will cloud decision making and virtually guarantee failure.

JACK D. SCHWAGER

When you sell in desperation, you always sell cheap.

PETER LYNCH

I have seen many traders and investors not only fail to assess the market, but then exacerbate the error by refusing to admit that they were wrong. "The market is wrong," they say. The fact is, the market is never wrong. Only we are wrong for failing to assess it properly.

DEAN LUNDELL

Letting your losses run is the most serious mistake made by almost all investors! You positively must accept that mistakes in either timing or selection of stocks are going to be made by even the most professional investors. In fact, I would go so far as to say if you aren't willing to cut short and take your losses, then you probably should not buy stocks. Would you drive your car down the street without brakes?

WILLIAM J. O'NEIL

Yes, risk-taking is inherently failure-prone. Otherwise, it would be called sure-thing-taking.

TIM MCMAHON

If you can't take a small loss, sooner or later you will take the mother of all losses.

JACK D. SCHWAGER

If I can't afford to take losses, I have no business at the gambling table or at the Casino of Wall Street. Wall Street is not a philanthropic organization. I walk into the Casino with my eyes open as I would if I were walking into a Casino in Las Vegas. I ignore the chatter, I watch the action, and I try my luck.

NICOLAS DARVAS

Never average a loss—don't add to a losing position. "Averaging down" is nothing more than a rationalization either to avoid admitting being wrong or to hope to recover losses against all odds.

VICTOR SPERANDEO

Guard particularly against being overeager to trade in order to win back prior losses. Vengeance trading is a sure recipe for failure.

JACK D. SCHWAGER

Don't hang onto a stock for sentimental reason or to escape payment of the capital gains tax. When a time to sell is indicated—*sell*! You'll make mistakes, of course—everybody does; success in this business is in being 90 percent right 70 percent of the time!

IRA U. COBLEIGH AND PETER J. DEANGELIS

I don't think you can consistently be a winning trader if you're banking on being right more than 50 percent of the time. You have to figure out how to make money being right only 20 to 30 percent of the time.

BILL LIPSCHUTZ

Perhaps my number one rule is: Don't try to make a profit on a bad trade, just try to find the best place to get out.

LINDA BRADFORD RASCHKE

One must simply get out while the getting is good. The secret is to hop off the elevator on one of the floors on the way up. In the stock market one good profit in hand is worth two on paper.

WILLIAM J. O'NEIL

A stock market decline is as routine as a January blizzard in Colorado. If you're prepared, it can't hurt you. A decline is a great opportunity to pick up the bargains left behind by investors who are fleeing the storm in panic.

PETER LYNCH

Some pundits advise selling if a stock declines 10 percent from your cost. Ridiculous! Either you understand the company or you don't. If you don't, you shouldn't own it. If you do, and if the decline is a typical market jiggle, then the logical maneuver is, if anything, to buy a bit more. If you're going to sell every time the stock goes down, you will never win, any more than a general who always retreats when the enemy advances.

JOHN TRAIN

I've always detested "stop orders".... Show me a portfolio with 10 percent stops, and I'll show you a portfolio that's destined to lose exactly that amount. When you put in a stop, you're admitting that you're going to sell the stock for less than it's worth today.

PETER LYNCH

TOPS AND BOTTOMS

The beginning of a price move is usually hard to trade because you're not sure whether you're right about the direction of the trend. The end is hard because people start taking profits and the market gets very choppy. The middle of the move is what I call the easy part. . . . I never try to buy a bottom or sell a top. Even if you manage to pick the bottom, the market can end up sitting there for years and tying up your capital. You don't want to have a position before a move has started. You want to wait until the move is already under way before you get into the market.

RANDY MCKAY

Fishing for tops and bottoms is an expensive trait. Usually, so many mistakes are made along the way that little or no money is left for the anticipated trend when it does actually show up.

HENRY CLASING

Bottom fishing is a popular investor pastime, but it's usually the fisherman who gets hooked. Trying to catch the bottom on a falling stock is like trying to catch a falling knife. It's normally a good idea to wait until the knife hits the ground and sticks, then vibrates for a while and settles down before you try to grab it. Grabbing a rapidly falling stock results in painful surprises, because inevitably you grab it in the wrong place.

PETER LYNCH

I never buy at the bottom and I always sell too soon.

BARON ROTHSCHILD

The investor with a portfolio of sound stocks should expect their prices to fluctuate and should neither be concerned by sizable declines nor become excited by sizable advances. He should always remember that market quotations are there for his convenience, either to be taken advantage of or to be ignored. He should never buy a stock *because* it has gone up or sell one *because* it has gone down. He would not be far wrong if this motto read more simply: "Never buy a stock immediately after a substantial rise or sell one immediately after a substantial drop."

BENJAMIN GRAHAM

In only a tiny minority of your trades will you ever pick the exact primo exit price, selling out a whole position just before the stock (or the overall market) tanks. The majority of the time, your stock will uptick over your sell price at least once in the ensuing few months after selling. Experienced investors should know this and not worry about it, but to a certain extent none of us can help looking over our shoulder to see if some old stock might be gaining on us.

DAVID AND TOM GARDNER

A long list of losers from my own portfolio constantly reminds me that the so-called smart money is exceedingly dumb about 40 percent of the time.

PETER LYNCH

The stock market is the one place where the high achiever is routinely shown up. It's easy to get an F here.

PETER LYNCH

Repeatedly ... I have sold a stock while it still was rising—and that has been one reason why I have held onto my fortune. Many a time, I might have made a good deal more by holding a stock, but I would also have been caught in the fall when the price of the stock collapsed.

BERNARD BARUCH

If you are in the right thing at the wrong time, you may be right but have a long wait; at least you are better off than coming late to the party. You don't want to be on the dance floor when the music stops.

"ADAM SMITH"

I try to wait until things set up just right before I take a trade. Then, when I'm ready to take the trade, I slowly count to ten before I pick up the phone. It's better to have the wrong idea and good timing than the right idea and bad timing.

LINDA BRADFORD RASCHKE

The principal thing that makes stocks go, in my opinion, is early discovery. . . . Our job is to capture the companies early-on in that huge growth phase, when you've got only two or three regional firms following it.

SCOTT STERLING JOHNSTON

A Trend is a Trend is a Trend until it stops being a Trend.

"ADAM SMITH"

Trade with the trend. "The trend is your friend." This is probably the most well-known rule of all. But as simple as it seems, it is easier to violate than you might think. Remember, there are three trends—the short-term, the intermediate term, and the long-term. Each trend is moving all the time and may be going in a direction opposing the other two. . . . Know which trend you are involved in and its correlation with the other two.

VICTOR SPERANDEO

It has taken me years to unlearn everything I was taught and I probably haven't succeeded yet. I cite this only because most of what has been written about the market tells you the way it ought to be, and the successful investors I know do not hold to the way it ought to be, they simply go with what is.

"ADAM SMITH"

I'm convinced that it's the cultural memory of the 1929 Crash more than any other single factor that continues to keep millions of investors away from stocks and attracts them to bonds and to money-market accounts. Sixty years later, the Crash is still scaring people out of stocks, including people in my generation who weren't even born in 1929. If this is a post-Crash trauma syndrome we suffer from, it's been very costly. All the people who've kept their money in bonds, money-market accounts, savings accounts or CDs to avoid being involved in another Crash have missed out on 60 years of stock-market gains and have suffered the ravages of inflation, which over time has done more damage to their wealth than another crash would have done, had they experienced one.

PETER LYNCH

The stock market has called nine of the last five recessions.

PAUL A. SAMUELSON

Buy cheap and sell dear.

BARON ROTHSCHILD

Timing is vital! It is much more important to buy cheap than to sell dear.

IRA U. COBLEIGH AND
PETER J. DEANGELIS

One market paradigm that I take exception to is: Buy low and sell high. I believe that far more money is made buying high and selling at even higher prices. That means buying stocks that have already had good moves and have high relative strength— that is, stocks in demand by other investors.

RICHARD DRIEHAUS

THE RANDOM WALK

Even a dart-throwing chimpanzee can select
a portfolio that performs as well as one carefully
selected by the experts.

BURTON G. MALKIEL

It's no secret on Wall Street that most fund
managers would look like geniuses if they simply
invested in a stock market index, turned out the
lights, and went home.

JIM JORGENSEN

No scientific evidence has yet been assembled to indicate that the investment performance of professionally managed portfolios as a group has been any better than that of randomly selected portfolios. Many people ask me how this thesis—first published in 1973—has held up. The answer is, "Very well indeed." While there continue to be some exceptions to the thesis, as I freely admitted in 1973, history has been very kind to random walkers. In the twenty-year period to 1994, over two-thirds of the professionals who manage mutual-fund common-stock portfolios were outperformed by the unmanaged Standard & Poor's 500-Stock Index.

BURTON G. MALKIEL

The markets are not random, because they are based on human behavior, and human behavior, especially mass behavior, is not random. It never has been, and it probably never will be.

JACK D. SCHWAGER

Markets do not move totally at random. They move because somebody decides to do something. People move markets. And powerful people move them powerfully. When stocks shoot down or up, it is usually because of actions taken in Washington, or Tokyo, or Bonn.

JAMES DALE DAVIDSON

It is a cold, austere world, the world of the random walk, and a negative one. The random walkers do believe in the intrinsic value of a stock, but they have not much help for us on that because a stock only sells for its intrinsic value—whatever that is—whenever the market rushes past it either optimistically or pessimistically, so that intrinsic value is right like a stopped clock is right twice a day.

"ADAM SMITH"

An amateur who devotes a small amount of study to companies in an industry he or she knows something about can outperform 95 percent of the paid experts who manage the mutual funds, plus have fun in doing it.

PETER LYNCH

Many people make the mistake of thinking that market behavior is truly predictable. Nonsense. Trading in the markets is an odds game, and the object is to always keep the odds in your favor.

VICTOR SPERANDEO

There is no System in the market, and there are many approaches that work.

"ADAM SMITH"

No one has yet learned how to put emotions into serial correlation coefficients and analysis of runs. It is absolutely true that statistically the price of a stock has no relation tomorrow to what it was yesterday. But people—the Crowd—do have a memory that extends from day to day.

"ADAM SMITH"

So now I have this 800 number, and if I ever have the urge to buy an airline stock, I dial this number and I say my name is Warren and I'm an airoholic. Then this guy talks me down on the other end.

WARREN BUFFETT

Make use of defensive measures such as options, futures, and other hedge vehicles if you are so inclined. Use protective stop loss orders; it is better to take a small loss at first than a large one later. Live to fight another day.

DEAN LUNDELL

My tendency has been to buy stocks, all a-tremble as I do so. Then when they show a profit I sell them, exultantly. (But never within six months, of course. I'm no anarchist.) It seems to me at these moments that I have achieved life's loveliest guerdon—making some money without doing any work. Then a long time later it turns out that I should have just bought them, and thereafter I should have just sat on them like a fat, stupid peasant. A peasant, however, who is rich beyond his limited dreams of avarice.

FRED SCHWED, JR.

In my opinion, the greatest misconception is the idea that if you buy and hold stocks for long periods of time, you'll always make money.

VICTOR SPERANDEO

The strongest emotions in the marketplace are greed and fear. In rising markets, you can almost feel the greed tide begin. . . . The greed itch begins when you see stocks move that you don't own. Then friends of yours have a stock that has doubled; or, if you have one that has doubled, they have one that has tripled. This is what produces bull market tops. Obviously no one rationally would want to buy at the top, and yet enough people do to produce a top. . . . The same thing happens in reverse. No matter what role the investor has started with, in a climax on one side or the other the role melts into the crowd role of greed or fear.

"ADAM SMITH"

TRADING

It's important to distinguish between respect for the market and fear of the market. While it's essential to respect the market to assure preservation of capital, you can't win if you're fearful of losing. Fear will keep you from making correct decisions.

HOWARD SEIDLER

Avoid "jogging in place" with your portfolio. Failure to decide is, in effect, a decision. If you would not care to buy each holding in your portfolio each day, you should sell it (barring tax considerations).

BENNETT W. GOODSPEED

Some of the best trades come when everyone gets very panicky. The crowd can often act very stupidly in the markets. You can picture price fluctuations around an equilibrium level as a rubber band being stretched—if it gets pulled too far, eventually it will snap back. As a short-term trader, I try to wait until the rubber band is stretched to its extreme point.

LINDA BRADFORD RASCHKE

There are only two emotions in Wall Street: fear and greed.

WILLIAM M. LEFEVRE, JR.

It would be foolish to overlook the human vice of greed. The successful trader must be able to recognize and control his greed. If you get a buzz from profits and depressed by losses, you belong in Las Vegas, not the markets.

MARK RITCHIE

A bull may make money, a bear may make money, but a pig, never!

ANONYMOUS

The markets that go wild are the ones with the best opportunity. Traditionally, what happens in a market that goes berserk is that even veteran traders will tend to stand aside. That's your opportunity to make the money. As the saying goes, "If you can keep your head about you while others are losing theirs, you can make a fortune."

MARK RITCHIE

Traders come from all walks of life. You don't have to be a rocket scientist to be a trader. In fact, some of the best traders whom I knew down on the floor were surf bums. Formal education didn't really seem to have much to do with a person's skill as a trader.

LINDA BRADFORD RASCHKE

In the real estate market, quality is determined by three measures: location, location, location. Three measures also can be applied to quality in the stock market: performance, performance, performance. Financial performance is the first measure of quality.... Production performance is the second measure.... Investment performance, as reflected in long-term capital gains and dividend growth, is the third measure.

GERALDINE WEISS AND GREGORY WEISS

Morning markets are the most active and the most liquid. They are largely public. Midday markets are thin and quiet. Most markets get more active and liquid in the afternoon prior to the close, but the activity is largely institutional.

DEAN LUNDELL

The most liquid period is the opening. Liquidity starts falling off pretty quickly after the opening. The second most liquid time of day is the close. Trading volume typically forms a U-shaped curve throughout the day. There's a lot of liquidity right at the opening, it then falls off, reaching a nadir at midday, and then it starts to climb back up, reaching a secondary peak on the close. Generally speaking, this pattern holds in almost every market. It's actually pretty amazing.

MONROE TROUT

I never trade at midday or in a quiet market. It is a great place to be ambushed.

DEAN LUNDELL

A successful trader is rational, analytical, able to control emotions, practical, and profit oriented.

MONROE TROUT

Any successful market approach will become too popular. The rate of return then declines, or "regresses to the mean."

JOHN TRAIN

It is too simple to say that a stock is worth whatever people will pay for it, because what people are willing to pay for it depends, in turn, on what they think it is worth. It is a circular definition, used as a rationalization of financial foolishness rather than as a rational way to appraise value.

ANDREW TOBIAS

Value, in my mind, is a mirage. If you look at many of the statistical screens used by value managers, many of the companies listed are bankruptcy candidates. They may look attractive relative to book value and inventory value, but the numbers only tell one side of the story.

LAURA J. SLOATE

Only a fool thinks price and value are the same.

ANTONIO MACHADO

To know values is to know the meaning of the market.

CHARLES DOW

123

Everybody has some information. The function of the markets is to aggregate that information, evaluate it, and get it incorporated into prices. But if information, as I insist, is widely scattered and diffuse, most individuals are not going to have much information relative to the total. Most people might just as well buy a share of the whole market, which pools all the information, than delude themselves into thinking they know something the market doesn't. They can't be hurt by doing that, because the price they pay will indeed reflect society's best current information.

MERTON MILLER

I believe that only short-term price swings can be predicted with any precision. The accuracy of a prediction drops off dramatically, the more distant the forecast time. I'm a strong believer in chaos theory.

LINDA BRADFORD RASCHKE

Heisenberg Principle of Investment: You may know where the market is going, but you can't possibly know where it's going after that.

ARTHUR BLOCH

It is often much easier to tell what will happen to the price of a stock than how much time will elapse before it happens.

PHILIP A. FISHER

Never make forecasts, especially about the future.

SAM GOLDWYN

I used to be, in my youth, clairvoyant. I had this perfect ability to call market turns. But as I got older I found that long-term investing is the way to go.

CHARLES SCHWAB

A margin call is what alerts you to the fact that your life is going to hell and that you *never* should have gotten into the market when you did, let alone on margin.

ANDREW TOBIAS

THE EFFICIENT MARKET

The essence of the efficient market thing is, after all, as we in economics have always held: There's no free lunch. You can't just sit back in your office scanning the newspapers, reading research reports, and listening to "Wall Street Week," and hope to earn above-normal rates of return. To beat the market you'll have to invest serious bucks to dig up information *no one else has yet*.

MERTON MILLER

Here is the conclusion I have arrived at: The market is not perfectly efficient at all times. However, the market is *constantly in the process of becoming efficient*. By that, I mean it takes time for efficiency to be achieved. The notion that information is reflected in stock prices instantaneously just doesn't seem to hold up.

PETER J. TANOUS

There are inefficiencies in the market every day. Our experience suggests that about 9% of the universe is inefficiently priced on any given day.

ROBERT B. GILLAM

If six out of ten of my stocks perform as expected, then I'm thankful. Six out of ten is all it takes to produce an enviable record on Wall Street.

PETER LYNCH

From a practical point of view, investors are probably better off if they just assume that markets are efficient. . . . It's one thing to say that markets are generally efficient. We have to add a second thing which is that, in any well-functioning market, the only thing investors get compensated for is taking risk. If people need to lay off some risk, they are going to have to compensate the people who will take that risk.

REX SINQUEFIELD

If you look at ten companies you'll find one that's interesting. If you look at 20, you'll find two; if you look at 100, you'll find ten. The person that turns over the most rocks wins the game.

PETER LYNCH

If the job has been correctly done when a common stock is purchased, the time to sell it is— almost never.

PHILIP A. FISHER

What always impresses me is how much better the relaxed, long-term owners of stocks do with their portfolios than the traders do with their switching of inventory. The relaxed investor is usually better informed and more understanding of essential values; he is more patient and less emotional; he pays smaller annual capital gains taxes; he does not incur unnecessary brokerage commissions; and he avoids behaving like Cassius by "thinking too much."

LUCIEN O. HOOPER

Management of one's emotional state is critical. The truly exceptional traders can stand up to anything. Instead of getting emotional when things don't go their way, they remain calm and act in accordance with their approach. . . . Trading actually tends to attract people who are ill suited to the task—those who are enamored with making lots of money; people who are willing to take high risks; individuals who seek excitement or who react to the world with emotional intensity.

CHARLES FAULKNER

Keep emotion out of your stock decision-making process. Love your spouse, your children, but don't love your stocks. Just because they have been good to you in the past is no guarantee they will be good to you in the future.

ANNE E. BROWN

The most important thing to realize is simplistic: *The stock doesn't know you own it.* All those marvelous things, or those terrible things, that you feel about a stock, or a list of stocks, or an amount of money represented by a list of stocks, all of those things are unreciprocated by the stock or the group of stocks. You can be in love if you want to, but that piece of paper doesn't love you, and unreciprocated love can turn into masochism, narcissism, or, even worse, market losses and unreciprocated hate.

"ADAM SMITH"

It might sound a little silly to have a reminder saying *The Stock Doesn't Know You Own It* were it not for all the identity fuel provided by the market these days. You could almost sell these identities as buttons: I Am the Owner of IBM, My Stocks Are Up 80 Percent; Flying Tiger Has Been So Good to Me I Love It; You All Laughed When I Bought Solitron and Look at Me Now.

"ADAM SMITH"

It's not enough to simply have the insight to see something apart from the rest of the crowd, you also need to have the courage to act on it and to stay with it. It's very difficult to be different from the rest of the crowd the majority of the time, which by definition is what you're doing if you're a successful trader.

BILL LIPSCHUTZ

Markets change continuously and so must you. What worked last year, last month, or even last week may very well not work today.

DEAN LUNDELL

Many people think that trading can be reduced to a few rules. Always do this or always do that. To me, trading isn't about *always* at all; it is about each situation.

BILL LIPSCHUTZ

Sell when there is an *overabundance* of optimism. When everyone is bubbling optimism and running around trying to get everyone else to buy, they are fully invested. At this point, all they can do is talk. They can't push the market up anymore. It takes buying power to do that.

JACK DREYFUS

133

Theories usually lose you money. The more you believe your theory, the more you will lose.

HENRY CLASING

No traders worth their salt will tell you what they are going to do. They will tell you after their position is on so you can spread the word and help drive the market. Another tactic of the major players is to advertise one position while they take the other side so they can liquidate their holdings.

DEAN LUNDELL

The entire purpose of the vast enterprise known collectively as "the stock market" is, from the point of view of the men who run it, to churn up the greatest possible amount of buying and selling, so as to generate the greatest possible number of commissions.

NICOLAS DARVAS

Invest less at the end of the month. Brokers tend to push stocks at the end of the month in an effort to match or surpass their previous month's sales.

NANCY DUNNAN

The one bit of friendly advice which I didn't hear from my friendly broker was: "Do nothing. Get out of the market." That would be too much to expect. Brokers and their account executives are, like casino operators and croupiers, necessarily in business to make money. And on Wall Street, that means commissions.

NICOLAS DARVAS

One nugget of advice that I believe is valuable to anyone trading the markets is: Don't worry about what the markets are going to do, worry about what you are going to do in response to the markets.

MICHAEL CARR

Market analysis can always discover ample explanations, *after the fact*, as to why a given issue spurted upward or fell off. Rumor of a stock split, anticipated good news of higher earnings, Presidential heartburn, or rumors of a Cuban invasion—there is always something to say. But the truth is that the observations made at the end of the trading day are all in the nature of post mortems. And they are mostly rationalizations in any case. The truth is that the market behaves as *it* does because the gamblers behave as *they* do, and no one can know what they will do until they have done it.

NICOLAS DARVAS

For some reason, people take their cues from price action rather than from values. What doesn't work is when you start doing things that you don't understand or because they worked last week for somebody else. The dumbest reason in the world to buy a stock is because it's going up.

WARREN BUFFETT

Wait for January. In thirty-six out of forty-five years since 1950, as January went, so went the market. If Wall Street likes the President's annual State of the Union message and federal budget for the coming year, investor enthusiasm tends to buoy the market for the next twelve months.

NANCY DUNNAN

The market on income stocks moves far less spectacularly than on growth stocks, but you get a better average dividend income. And you sleep better.

MARY ELIZABETH SCHLAYER
AND MARILYN H. COOLEY

Invest in vanity. Buy stocks in high-profile companies whose products are designed to make you feel good and look good.

NANCY DUNNAN

I look at my portfolio as little puppy dogs. Some days they're well, some days they're sick, some days they leave you alone. But every day there's something going on.

LAURA J. SLOATE

There are too many unpredictable things that can happen within two months. To me, the ideal trade lasts ten days, but I approach every trade as if I'm only going to hold it two or three days.

LINDA BRADFORD RASCHKE

The risk of paying too high a price for good-quality stocks—while a real one—is not the chief hazard confronting the average buyer of securities. Observation over many years has taught us that the chief losses to investors come from the purchase of *low-quality* securities at times of favorable business conditions.

BENJAMIN GRAHAM

One of my favorite patterns is the tendency for the markets to move from relative lows to relative highs and vice versa every two to four days. This pattern is a function of human behavior. It takes several days of a market rallying before it looks really good. That's when everyone wants to buy it, and that's the time when the professionals, like myself, are selling. Conversely, when the market has been down for a few days, and everyone is bearish, that's the time I like to be buying.

LINDA BRADFORD RASCHKE

It is anticipation of growth rather than growth itself that makes for lively speculation and big profits in the so-called growth stocks.

NICOLAS DARVAS

Anybody who plays the market without inside information is like a man buying cows in the moonlight.

DAN DREW

139

There are old traders around and bold traders around, but there are no old, bold traders around.

BOB DINDA

The stock market is a state of mind. Resisting your natural impulses to be euphoric or full of panic when the media demand these reactions will be your first step toward profit.

JOHN D. SPOONER

As far as I'm concerned, the stock market doesn't exist. It is there only as a reference to see if anybody is offering to do anything foolish.

WARREN BUFFETT

THE SECURITIES AND EXCHANGE COMMISSION

I am willing to submit an idea to the Securities and Exchange Commission that perhaps they have thought of themselves: they are in the position of a doctor who has only one patient, with no prospect of ever getting another. It would be a tactical error to kill this patient, even though a commendable scientific zeal prompts the doctor to try out his whole shelf of pharmacopoeia on him. After all, there is no real danger in this case of the patient ever becoming completely cured.

FRED SCHWED, JR.

I have at times fancied that I detected in the S.E.C. a spirit of gleeful vengeance, which should not be the attitude of a regulatory body. A police force is supposed to keep a city orderly. Destroying the city is not among its duties. . . . I find myself wishing that the Commission would perform its functions with a little less zip and hurrah. Could they not model their procedure and publicity a little closer to that of the Department of Weights and Measures, and a little less to that of the G-men looking for a Public Enemy?

FRED SCHWED, JR.

DIVIDENDS

A cow for her milk,
A hen for her eggs,
And a stock, by heck,
For her dividends.

WALL STREET RHYME

Dividends are truly the jumper cables of the investment world.

JIM JORGENSEN

Don't mail me any more proxies, please.
Tell me, incorporated tease,
Why don't you save the stamps and send,
Once in a while, a dividend?

MARGARET FISHBACK

Approximately 75% of the companies traded
on the New York Stock Exchange pay cash dividends
to their shareholders. It is perhaps the most sacred of
all corporate financial components, and the measure
of value we hold in the highest regard.

GERALDINE WEISS AND
GREGORY WEISS

Reinvesting your dividends in a stock
mutual fund is the glue that holds your financial
plan together.

JIM JORGENSEN

Some investors live or die by earnings reports. Earnings are important, but who knows if the reported earnings are accurate? ...A clever accountant can make earnings appear good or not so good, depending on the season or the objective. There can be no subterfuge about a cash dividend. It is either paid or it is not paid. If it is paid, the shareholder knows that the company is making money. If it is not paid, no rhetoric can disguise the circumstances.

GERALDINE WEISS AND
GREGORY WEISS

Fake realism is the escapist literature of our time. And probably the ultimate escapist reading is that masterpiece of total unreality, the daily stock market report.

URSULA K. LEGUIN

Dividends don't lie.

GERALDINE WEISS AND JANET LOWE

SPECULATING

Speculation is an effort, probably unsuccessful, to turn a little money into a lot. Investment is an effort, which should be successful, to prevent a lot of money from becoming little.

FRED SCHWED, JR.

If a speculator is correct half of the time, he is hitting a good average. Even being right three or four times out of 10 should yield a person a fortune if he has the sense to cut his losses quickly on the ventures where he has been wrong.

BERNARD BARUCH

Investment and speculation are said to be two different things, and the prudent man is advised to engage in the one and avoid the other. This is something like explaining to the troubled adolescent that Love and Passion are two different things. He perceives that they are different, but they don't seem quite different enough to clear up his problems.

FRED SCHWED, JR.

The most realistic distinction between the investor and the speculator is found in their attitude toward stock-market movements. The speculator's primary interest lies in anticipating and profiting from market fluctuations. The investor's primary interest lies in acquiring and holding suitable securities at suitable prices.

BENJAMIN GRAHAM

Gambling is taking a risk when the odds are against you, like playing the lottery or pumping silver dollars into a slot machine. Speculating is taking a risk when the odds are in your favor.

VICTOR SPERANDEO

If, instead of playing the horses, an individual chooses to play the market, that is his own affair. Only he must understand that speculating in stocks is gambling, not investing.

CATHERINE CROOK DE CAMP

There are two times in a man's life when he should not speculate: when he can't afford it, and when he can.

MARK TWAIN

The term *speculation* has, in my opinion, gained an unearned negative connotation. People think of speculators as the people who drive prices up in shady stock transactions, real estate deals, and so forth. But in reality, all market speculators do is focus their attention on intermediate price movements, trying to profit by their buying and selling activity. Speculators provide crucial liquidity to the markets and in most cases facilitate the orderly transfer of assets to their best use.

VICTOR SPERANDEO

The spirit of risk-taking lies deep within human nature. The hope of hitting the jackpot is what has differentiated the human race from an ant heap. For all his trickery, his tragic and comic misadventures, the speculator has been a vital mainspring of the human experience.

DANA L. THOMAS

People say, "One great speculation is worth a lifetime of prudent investing"—a terrific line, and true. The problem comes in finding the great speculation. Few people ever do, particularly if they are amateurs. The line I prefer: "In the financial marketplace, you get what you pay for, if you're careful. If you try to get more, you get burned."

ANDREW TOBIAS

FINANCIAL ADVICE

Bulls and bears aren't responsible for as many stock losses as bum steers.

OLIN MILLER

The cheapest commodity in the world is investment advice from people not qualified to give it.

LOUIS ENGEL

Possibly the only thing worse than an amateur investor is an amateur investment adviser.

NICOLAS DARVAS

The odds of anyone calling you on the phone with good investment advice are about the same as winning Lotto without buying a ticket.

JOEL GREENBLATT

Give a cold shoulder to cold callers. Never invest in anything based on a phone call from someone you don't know or whose office is a post office box.

NANCY DUNNAN

Those who make quick, spectacular profits usually lose them and more on other mistakes. Don't be awed by anyone's record.

HARRY BROWNE

If you ever find yourself tempted to seek out someone else's opinion on a trade, that's usually a sure sign that you should get out of your position.

LINDA BRADFORD RASCHKE

"Trade with the trend, not your friend." . . .
Just in terms of odds, when you consider the
hundreds of thousands of people involved in the
markets, what do you think the chances are that one
of your acquaintances knows something that the rest
of the world doesn't? If he or she really *does* know
something, then the chances are that it is "inside"
information, and trading on inside information is
illegal. But 999 times out of 1000, the so-called "tip"
is just someone else's opinion.

VICTOR SPERANDEO

Here is what to do with hot tips. If you get a
hot tip, make a note of it and pretend to be very
interested. But don't buy. If the thing takes off, listen a
little more closely the next time this fellow has a tip.
If it gets mauled, look bitter the next time you see
him. He will assume that you bought the stock; he
will feel guilty; and he will buy you a very nice lunch.

ANDREW TOBIAS

The Internet and other on-line services have hundreds of chat rooms, message boards, news groups, and so forth. Besides being a regulatory nightmare for the government, these chat rooms, news groups, message boards, and so forth are either full of amateurs with enough knowledge to be dangerous, or other people hyping something to help drive a position they already have. Be very skeptical of what you read or hear.

DEAN LUNDELL

Consistent winners tell virtually no one their activities in the marketplace. . . . Consistent losers tell anyone who will listen the details of their market activities, to the point of campaigning for their point of view.

HENRY CLASING

If you heard that a young kid, or maybe a plumber, had come up with a neat way to perform appendectomies, would you buy his book and give it a try? Or would you stick with a medical doctor? Why is it that when it comes to investing, anyone who is a bit successful thinks he or she can tell you how to do it better than the professionals who devote their lives to it?

PETER J. TANOUS

Some extremely sharp investment advisers can get you in at the bottom of the market. Some extremely sharp ones can get you out at the top. They are never the same people.

GARY NORTH

To be successful an advisory service must tell people what they *want to hear*, not necessarily what the truth is.

NICOLAS DARVAS

The broker influences the customer with his knowledge of the future, but only after he has convinced himself. The worst that should be said of him is that he wants to convince *himself* badly and that he therefore succeeds in convincing himself—generally badly.

FRED SCHWED, JR.

If the reason people invest is to make money, then in seeking advice they are asking others to tell them how to make money. That idea has some element of naïveté. Businessmen seek professional advice on various elements of their business, but they do not expect to be told how to make a profit. That is their own bailiwick. When they, or nonbusiness people, rely on others to make *investment profits* for them, they are expecting a kind of result for which there is no true counterpart in ordinary business affairs.

BENJAMIN GRAHAM

156

Wall Street is the only place that people ride to in a Rolls Royce to get advice from those who take the subway.

WARREN BUFFETT

There are two ways to really know people. One is to live with them; the other is to handle their money.

JOHN D. SPOONER

If your investment adviser plays golf, ask him what his handicap is. If it is under six, be careful; the chances are he is either lying or spending far too much time on the golf course.

BENNETT W. GOODSPEED

If you're uncomfortable with your financial adviser, it's probably with good reason.

NANCY DUNNAN

Learn from the mistakes of others. You won't live long enough to make them all yourself.

JANE BRYANT QUINN

By and large you should manage your own money. No one is going to care about it as much as you. And no one but you is going to manage it for free.

ANDREW TOBIAS

BANKS

There have been three great inventions since the beginning of time: fire, the wheel, and central banking.

WILL ROGERS

Everyone needs a small-town banker. Especially in a big town.

JANE BRYANT QUINN

The process by which banks create money is so simple that the mind is repelled. When something so important is involved, a deeper mystery seems only decent. . . . The discovery that banks could so create money came very early in the development of banking. There was that interest to be earned. Where such reward is waiting, men have a natural instinct for innovation.

JOHN KENNETH GALBRAITH

Visiting the banker always makes the list of life's sweaty-palmed experiences. Stripping down to have your financials examined is submitting to an emotional proctoscopy that no amount of "friendly banker" advertising is ever going to change.

HARVEY MACKAY

A bank is a place that will lend you money if you can prove you don't need it.

BOB HOPE

The trouble with most banks is that the person who writes the bank's advertising is not the same person who makes the loans.

ANONYMOUS

Risk-taking in banking is incompetence. If you feel that banks should take risks with their money then you probably have a misconception of what the function of a bank is.

MICHAEL PHILLIPS

A sound banker is not one who foresees danger and avoids it, but one who, when he is ruined, is ruined in a conventional and orthodox way so that no one can really blame him.

JOHN MAYNARD KEYNES

The conservative banker is an impressive specimen, diffusing the healthy glow which comes of moderation in eating, living, and thinking. He sits in state and spends his days saying, with varying inflections and varying contexts, "no." . . . He says "yes" only a few times a year. . . . His business might be defined as the lending of money exclusively to people who have no pressing need of it. In times of stress, when everybody needs money, he strives to avoid lending to anybody, but usually makes an exception of the United States government. Likewise, in prosperous times he is a mighty liberal lender—so liberal that years later unfriendly committees ask him what he thought he was thinking about, and he is unable to remember clearly.

FRED SCHWED, JR.

CREDIT

Beautiful credit! The foundation of modern society.

MARK TWAIN

Let us run up debts. One is nobody without debts.

MURIEL SPARK

Regiments are joining in the Master Charge
That's blowing up the G.N.P.
Hardly anybody now remains at large
Who lacks creditability.

FELICIA LAMPORT

The creditor hath a better memory
than the debtor.

JAMES HOWELL

Debt is the sort of Bedfellow who is forever
pulling all the Covers his way.

MINNA THOMAS ANTRIM

The growth of credit cards in the sixties and seventies blurred the distinction between convenience and debt. . . . Their enticing names, such as *Visa* and *Access*, carried none of the old associations of frowning bank managers saying no to a loan. With all their benevolence they could easily conceal their role as an extra overdraft with an abnormally high interest rate.

ANTHONY SAMPSON

Credit is the pavement along which production travels.

JOHN MAYNARD KEYNES

We at Chrysler borrow money the old-fashioned way. We pay it back.

LEE IACOCCA

165

ECONOMICS

If ignorance paid dividends, most Americans could make a fortune out of what they don't know about economics.

LUTHER H. HODGES

Television interviewers with a reputation for penetrating thought regularly begin interviews with economists with the question: "Now tell me, just what is money anyway?" The answers are invariably incoherent.

JOHN KENNETH GALBRAITH

There are only two areas where new ideas are terribly dangerous—economics and sex.

FELIX ROHATYN

We have become to some extent, I think, economic hypochondriacs. You get a wiggle in a statistic ... and everyone runs to get the thermometer.

PAUL W. McCRACKEN

Economics is not a science, in the sense that a policy can be repeatedly applied under similar conditions and will repeatedly produce similar results.

MILLICENT FENWICK

Economics limps along with one foot in untested hypotheses and the other in untestable slogans.

JOAN ROBINSON

167

One of the difficulties of economics is that it is too easy to explain, after a particular event has happened, why it should have happened; and too easy to explain, before it happens, why it should not happen.

M.G. KENDALL

I learned that economics was not an exact science and that the most erudite men would analyze the economic ills of the world and derive a totally different conclusion.

EDITH SUMMERSKILL

An economist is an expert who will know tomorrow why the things he predicted yesterday didn't happen.

EARL WILSON

If all economists were laid end to end, they would not reach a conclusion.

GEORGE BERNARD SHAW

Most economists, like doctors, are reluctant to make predictions, and those who make them are seldom accurate. The economy, like the human body, is a highly complex system whose workings are not thoroughly understood.

ALICE M. RIVLIN

An economist's guess is liable to be just as good as anybody else's.

WILL ROGERS

The only function of economic forecasting is to make astrology look respectable.

EZRA SOLOMON

169

The economy depends about as much on economists as the weather does on weather forecasters.

JEAN-PAUL KAUFFMANN

One of the soundest rules I try to remember when making forecasts in the field of economics is that whatever is to happen is happening already.

SYLVIA PORTER

A monetary system is like a liver: it does not take up very much of our thoughts when it goes right, but it attracts a great deal of attention when it goes wrong.

D.H. ROBERTSON

Monetary Theory, when all is said and done, is little more than a vast elaboration of the truth that "it all comes out in the wash."

JOHN MAYNARD KEYNES

Observation of realities has never, to put it mildly, been one of the strengths of economic development theory.

JANE JACOBS

In all recorded history there has not been one economist who had to worry about where the next meal was coming from.

PETER F. DRUCKER

There are three main causes that dispose men to madness: love, ambition, and the study of currency problems.

WALTER LEAF

[Economists' advice] is something like patent medicine—people know it is largely manufactured by quacks and that a good percentage of the time it won't work, but they continue to buy the brand whose flavor they like.

BARBARA BERGMANN

Economics is extremely useful as a form of employment for economists.

JOHN KENNETH GALBRAITH

STATISTICS

Torture numbers, and they'll confess
to anything.

GREGG EASTERBROOK

He uses statistics as a drunken man uses
lampposts—for support rather than for illumination.

ANDREW LANG

Don't believe the statistics unless you know
the statistician.

LYNNE ALPERN AND ESTHER BLUMENFELD

The average family exists only on paper and its average budget is a fiction, invented by statisticians for the convenience of statisticians.

SYLVIA PORTER

Statistics are human beings with the tears wiped off.

PAUL BRODEUR

Statistics show that of those who contract the habit of eating, very few ever survive.

WILLIAM WALLACE IRVIN

There are three kinds of lies: lies, damned lies, and statistics.

BENJAMIN DISRAELI

TAXES

Taxes are what we pay for civilized society.

OLIVER WENDELL HOLMES, JR.

Taxes, after all, are the dues that we pay
for the privilege of membership in an organized
society.

FRANKLIN D. ROOSEVELT

I'm proud to be paying taxes in the United States. The only thing is—I could be just as proud for half the money.

ARTHUR GODFREY

Psychiatrists say it's not good for man to keep too much to himself. The Internal Revenue Service says the same thing.

HAROLD SMITH

There's nothing wrong with waiting for your ship to come in, but you can be sure that if it ever does, the Receiver of Revenue will be right there to help you unload it.

DAVID BIGGS

If you make any money, the government shoves you in the creek once a year with it in your pockets, and all that doesn't get wet you can keep.

WILL ROGERS

People who complain about the tax system fall into two categories—men and women.

BARRY STEINER

Keeping your hard-earned dollars from taking a one-way trip to Washington is indeed a challenge . . . and one worthy of your most careful attention. Few other endeavors will add more to your net worth, since the only money you will ever have for investing and spending is what the government lets you keep.

VENITA VANCASPEL

177

Let me say at the outset, that if anyone doesn't hate high taxes . . . well, he just hasn't paid his taxes.

ADLAI STEVENSON

Anyone may so arrange his affairs that his taxes shall be as low as possible. He is not bound to choose that pattern which best pays the Treasury. Everyone does it, rich and poor alike, and all do right; for nobody owes any public duty to pay more than the law demands.

JUDGE LEARNED HAND

Anybody has a right to evade taxes if he can get away with it. No citizen has a moral obligation to assist in maintaining the government.

J.P. MORGAN

Day in and day out, your tax accountant can make or lose you more money than any single person in your life, with the possible exception of your kids.

HARVEY MACKAY

Even taxpayers who turn the dirty work over to accountants and other specialists should not simply wash their hands of the matter. Leaving taxes entirely to the experts can be hazardous to your wealth.

DEBORAH LOHSE

If Patrick Henry thought that taxation without representation was bad, he should see how bad it is with representation.

FARMER'S ALMANAC

I believe we should all pay our tax bill with a smile. I tried—but they wanted cash.

ANONYMOUS

Next to being shot at and missed, nothing is really quite as satisfying as an income tax refund.

F.J. RAYMOND

Noah must have taken into the Ark two taxes, one male and one female, and did they multiply bountifully! Next to guinea pigs, taxes must have been the most prolific animals.

WILL ROGERS

Today it takes more brains and effort to make out the income-tax form than it does to make the income.

ALFRED E. NEUMAN

The art of taxation consists in so plucking the goose as to obtain the largest possible amount of feathers with the smallest possible amount of hissing.

JEAN-BAPTISTE COLBERT

What is the difference between a taxidermist and a tax collector? The taxidermist takes only your skin.

MARK TWAIN

It has been said that one man's loophole is another man's livelihood. Even if this is true, it certainly is not fair, because the loophole-livelihood of those who are reaping undeserved benefits can be the economic noose of those who are paying more than they should.

MILLICENT FENWICK

Only the little people pay taxes.

LEONA HELMSLEY

The income tax presses more heavily on the possessors of small incomes than on the possessors of large incomes.

MILLICENT GARRETT FAWCETT

I'm a middle-bracket person with a middle-
bracket spouse
And we live together gaily in a middle-bracket
house.
We've a fair-to-middlin' family; we take the
middle view;
So we're manna sent from heaven to internal
revenue.

PHYLLIS McGINLEY

Why does a slight tax increase cost you two
hundred dollars and a substantial tax cut save you
thirty cents?

PEG BRACKEN

The income tax has made more liars out of the American people than golf has. Even when you make a tax form out on the level, you don't know when it is through if you are a crook or a martyr.

WILL ROGERS

Is there a phrase in the English language more fraught with menace than *a tax audit*?

ERICA JONG

The last important human activity not subject to taxation is sex.

RUSSELL BAKER

DEFINITIONS

A deficit is what you have when you haven't got as much as you had when you had nothing.

GERALD F. LIEBERMAN

B ankruptcy is a legal proceeding in which you put your money in your pants pocket and give your coat to your creditors.

JOEY ADAMS

Budget: a mathematical confirmation of your suspicions.

A.A. LATIMER

Inflation is too much money chasing too few goods.

BEN STEIN AND HERBERT STEIN

Inflation might be called prosperity with high blood pressure.

ARNOLD H. GLASOW

Inflation is the senility of democracies.

SYLVIA TOWNSEND WARNER

Inflation is the process that enables you to live in a more expensive neighborhood without going to the trouble of moving.

A.W. CLAUSSEN

The other man's money is *capital*; getting it is *labor*.

MARY PETTIBONE POOLE

Capital is that part of wealth which is devoted to obtaining further wealth.

ALFRED MARSHALL

WEALTH

Wealth is not without its advantages and the case to the contrary, although it has often been made, has never proved widely persuasive.

JOHN KENNETH GALBRAITH

Riches may not bring happiness, but neither does poverty.

SOPHIE IRENE LOEB

Although wealth may not bring happiness, the immediate prospect of it provides a wonderfully close imitation.

PATRICK O'BRIAN

Wealth ... gives you freedom to make choices.

OPRAH WINFREY

Most people have it all wrong about wealth in America. Wealth is not the same as income. If you make a good income each year and spend it all, you are not getting wealthier. You are just living high. Wealth is what you accumulate, not what you spend.

THOMAS J. STANLEY AND
WILLIAM D. DANKO

If a man has money, it is usually a sign, too, that he knows how to take care of it; don't imagine his money is easy to get simply because he has plenty of it.

EDGAR WATSON HOWE

The desire to obtain enough money to achieve one's desired standard of living is in the realm of realistic behavior. The desire to accumulate extreme wealth is irrational. Beyond a certain point, added wealth cannot increase the opulence of one's style of living or increase one's happiness.

HERB GOLDBERG AND ROBERT T. LEWIS

The love of wealth is therefore to be traced, as either a principal or accessory motive, at the bottom of all that the Americans do; this gives to all their passions a sort of family likeness.

ALEXIS DE TOCQUEVILLE

Let me tell you about the very rich. They are different from you and me.

F. SCOTT FITZGERALD

Yes, they have more money.

ERNEST HEMINGWAY

Contrary to F. Scott Fitzgerald's claim, the rich really *aren't* all that different from you and me—with one major exception: They're an awful lot more careful about how they spend and invest their money.

THOMAS J. STANLEY AND
WILLIAM D. DANKO

Let's face it: one way in which the rich *are* different is that they have access to the country's top financial minds.

JEAN SHERMAN CHATZKY

The rich aren't like us, they pay less taxes.

PETER DE VRIES

What are three words that profile the affluent? Frugal frugal frugal.

THOMAS J. STANLEY AND
WILLIAM D. DANKO

Once you are rich you are usually always rich. Money makes money.

ALFRED A. MONTAPERT

Abundance is in crucial ways a state of mind.

SUZE ORMAN

Abundance will never be a factor of how much money one has. Rather it is always a factor of how one *feels* about what money one *does* have.

STUART WILDE

Never in the history of the world have so many people been so rich; never in the history of the world have so many of those same people felt themselves so poor.

LEWIS H. LAPHAM

It's not a sin to be rich anymore, it's a miracle.

JOHN CONNALLY

If you know exactly how rich you are, you are not really rich.

JOHN PAUL GETTY

The wealth of a person should be estimated, not by the amount he has, but by the use he makes of it.

JOSH BILLINGS

Some people think they are worth a lot of money just because they have it.

FANNIE HURST

There are a handful of people whom money won't spoil, and we all count ourselves among them.

MIGNON McLAUGHLIN

MILLIONAIRES

A man who has a million dollars is as well off as if he were rich.

JOHN JACOB ASTOR

The danger is that when you have your million, you then want two, because you have a button saying I Am a Millionaire and that is who you are, and there are, all of a sudden—as you will notice—so many people with buttons saying I Am a Double Millionaire.

"ADAM SMITH"

I don't want to be a millionaire, I just want to live like one.

TOOTS SHOR

Despite increasing taxes, controls, and other barriers imposed by government agencies, the number of millionaires continues to grow to the point where one wit recently remarked, "Soon millionaires will be a dime a dozen." Still, the odds against someone who is poor or middle class becoming rich are much greater than those against the rich getting richer.

HERB GOLDBERG AND
ROBERT T. LEWIS

Eighty percent of America's millionaires are first-generation rich.

THOMAS J. STANLEY AND
WILLIAM D. DANKO

I'm opposed to millionaires, but it would be dangerous to offer me the position.

MARK TWAIN

It will be a great mistake for the community to shoot the millionaires, for they are the bees that make the most honey, and contribute most to the hive even after they have gorged themselves full. . . . Under our present conditions the millionaire who toils on is the cheapest article which the community secures at the price it pays for him, namely, his shelter, clothing, and food.

ANDREW CARNEGIE

REAL ESTATE

The highest yield you can get on an investment in the United States is in real estate.

MARY ELIZABETH SCHLAYER
AND MARILYN H. COOLEY

Buy land. They're not making it anymore.

WILL ROGERS

Will Rogers is often quoted as saying that he favored investing in land "because they aren't making any more of it." Will should have stuck to being a comedian instead of turning investment adviser, although I'll admit some people think there isn't any difference.

MICHAEL K. EVANS

Everyone said, "You can't lose money in real estate, because they're not making any more of it." Hmmmm. Where did everyone go wrong?

JANE BRYANT QUINN

The three most important rules in selecting the right piece of real estate are location, location, location (and when we have periods of tight money I would add terms, terms, terms).

VENITA VANCASPEL

The old timers in real estate used to say there are three and only three rules for a successful real estate deal. They are (1) location, (2) location, and (3) location. To this I say horsefeathers, horsefeathers, and horsefeathers. At one time this was possibly the law that led to success. But in today's market of high financing costs and mobile population, the rules have changed.

MARK OLIVER HAROLDSEN

For all the huffing and puffing of the doubters, a home of our own is still the rock on which our hopes are built. Price appreciation aside (and most houses *will* appreciate, eventually), home-ownership is a state of mind. It's your piece of the earth. It's where a family's toes grow roots. It's where the flowers are yours, not God's.

JANE BRYANT QUINN

INSURANCE

Life insurance can be numbingly complicated. Clients often turn off their brains and surrender their judgment to the very agent or planner who brought on their coma in the first place.

JANE BRYANT QUINN

Auto insurance is a toll bridge, over which every honest driver has to pass.

JANE BRYANT QUINN

RETIREMENT

If you want to build a realistic retirement nest egg, you have to marry the stock market as soon as you can and stick with it for the rest of your life.

JIM JORGENSEN

You can be young without money but you can't be old without it.

TENNESSEE WILLIAMS

In youth money is a convenience, an aid to pleasure. In age it is an absolute necessity, for when we are old we have to buy even consideration and politeness from those about us.

DOROTHY DIX

It's daring and challenging to be young and poor, but never to be old and poor. Whatever resources of good health, character, and fortitude you bring to retirement, remember, also, to bring money.

JANE BRYANT QUINN

I have enough money to last me the rest of my life, unless I buy something.

ANONYMOUS

Gone today, here tomorrow.

CATHERINE CROOK DE CAMP,
ON RETIREMENT SAVINGS

I can't take it with me I know
But will it last until I go?

MARTHA F. NEWMEYER

The three immutable facts: You own stuff.
You will die. Someone will get that stuff.

JANE BRYANT QUINN

Attitudes Toward Money

The way in which we manage the business of getting and spending is closely tied to our personal philosophy of living. We begin to develop this philosophy long before we have our first dollar to spend; and unless we are thinking people, our attitude toward money management may continue through the years to be tinged with the ignorance and innocence of childhood.

CATHERINE CROOK DE CAMP

I believe that one's basic financial attitudes are—like a tendency toward fat knees—probably formed *in utero*, or, at the very latest, *in cribbo*.

PEG BRACKEN

Money usually represents so much more than dollars and cents. It is tied up with our deepest emotional needs: for love, power, security, independence, control, self-worth.

OLIVIA MELLAN

Money is a mirror. An examination of your money and the way you use money is a way of understanding yourself in the same way that a mirror provides a way of seeing yourself.

MICHAEL PHILLIPS

Money is a metaphor and a reality. It provides choices but demands self-knowledge from us: We must decide what we are willing or unwilling to do for money.

SARA ANN FRIEDMAN

What we do with money—how we use it, earn it, think about it, protect it, donate it, spend it, invest it and preserve it—*is nothing more than a metaphor for how we feel inside*.

REBECCA MADDOX

There isn't a part of our lives that money doesn't touch—it affects our relationships, the way we go about our everyday activities, our ability to make dreams reality, everything.

SUZE ORMAN

Wanting money is an acceptable attitude. Learning to accept reality and make the most of what you have is also an acceptable attitude. Money is a way to make the world work for us; money also gives us the power to change things. It is okay to *prosper*. The total amount of money you have is not the significant item—the attitude you have about it is.

BARBARA PATTERSON, NANCY MEADOWS,
CAROL DREGER

Our right or wrong use of money is the utmost test of character, as well as the root of happiness or misery, throughout our whole lives.

DINAH MULOCK CRAIK

In the planning stages of this global survey it was hoped that somewhere in the world a nation would be found whose people are poor but happy. We didn't find such a place.

GEORGE GALLUP

The relationship between money and happiness has been debated for centuries. Phrases like, "The best things in life are free," "Money can't buy happiness," and "They were poor but happy," have been bantered about for so long and so often that they have been all but accepted as true.

HERB GOLDBERG AND
ROBERT T. LEWIS

People invariably have scapegoats, and money has always been one of the most convenient ones—because it is commonly agreed that we can't do most of the things we want to do because we don't have enough money. As long as the majority of us believe that, it may be a useful, convenient mirage.

MICHAEL PHILLIPS

Despite evidence everywhere to the contrary, millions of people seem to think that money is the panacea that will solve most of their problems. And if a little bit of money doesn't do the trick, they are convinced that more money will.

HERB GOLDBERG AND ROBERT T. LEWIS

A poor person who is unhappy is in a better position than a rich person who is unhappy. Because the poor person has hope. He thinks money would help.

JEAN KERR

Empty pockets never held anyone back. It's only empty heads and empty hearts that do it.

NORMAN V. PEALE

True financial freedom doesn't depend on how much money you have. Financial freedom is when you have power over your fears and anxieties instead of the other way around.

SUZE ORMAN

To the extent that a person is obsessed with the possession and accumulation of money to the exclusion of how money is acquired—when the satisfaction in *having* money submerges the satisfaction derived from the *process of making* money—then it can be said that the person has an unhealthy attachment to money.

HERB GOLDBERG AND
ROBERT T. LEWIS

Almost everyone is uncomfortable talking about money.

OLIVIA MELLAN

Money is meant not for hoarding, but for using; the aim of life should be to use it in the right way—to spend as much as we can lawfully spend, both upon ourselves and others. And sometimes it is better to do this in our lifetime, when we can see that it is well spent, than to leave it to the chance spending of those that come after us.

DINAH MULOCK CRAIK

Millions of people apparently worship money. Even more dream about having millions of dollars and fantasize about the things they would do with it. It is probably safe to say that money is as much a preoccupation with most people as is sex. Yet, the primary reason that more people do not have more money is that, despite their longing, money is really not worth what it would take to get it.

HERB GOLDBERG AND
ROBERT T. LEWIS

212

The dollar sign is the only sign in which the modern man appears to have any real faith.

HELEN ROWLAND

Money does not corrupt people. What corrupts people is lack of affection. . . . Money is simply the bandage which wounded people put over their wounds.

MARGARET HALSEY

A person who is careless about money is careless about everything, and untrustworthy in everything.

DINAH MULOCK CRAIK

Money can be translated into the beauty of living, a support in misfortune, an education, or future security. It also can be translated into a source of bitterness.

SYLVIA PORTER

213

People's feelings about themselves change when they change the way they handle their money. Once they begin treating their money with respect, their self-respect shoots up as well.

SUZE ORMAN

As our net worth falls, so does our self-worth. Ironically, it's when we don't have it that we most feel we have to flaunt it.

SUZE ORMAN

To aspire to riches is as American as apple pie. To *fear affluence* is also part of American tradition.

HERB GOLDBERG AND
ROBERT T. LEWIS

If a man runs after money, he's money-mad; if he keeps it, he's a capitalist; if he spends it, he's a playboy; if he doesn't get it, he's a ne'er-do-well; if he doesn't try to get it, he lacks ambition. If he gets it without working for it, he's a parasite; and if he accumulates it after a lifetime of hard work, people call him a fool who never got anything out of life.

VIC OLIVER

The worship of money and the condemnation of money exist side by side, sometimes even within the same individual.

HERB GOLDBERG AND ROBERT T. LEWIS

"What should I do with $1,000,000?" is not very different from "What should I do with my life?" (If you could deal with only one question, which would you take?)

MICHAEL PHILLIPS

Library of Congress Cataloging-in-Publication Data

Money talks : quotations on money and investing / compiled by Rosalie
Maggio.
p.   cm.
ISBN 0-7352-0015-7 (cloth)
1. Money—Quotations, maxims, etc.   2. Investments—Quotations,
maxims, etc.   I. Maggio, Rosalie.
PN6084.M56M67   1998
332.4—dc21   98-17898
                                                                      CIP

ISBN 0-7352-0015-7

Text design: *Suzanne Behnke*

Excerpts from *The New Beacon Book of Quotations by Women*
(Boston: Beacon Press, 1996) are reprinted with permission.

PRENTICE HALL PRESS
Paramus, NJ 07652

A Simon & Schuster Company

On the World Wide Web at http://www.phdirect.com

Prentice Hall International (UK) Limited, *London*
Prentice Hall of Australia Pty. Limited, *Sydney*
Prentice Hall of Canada, Inc., *Toronto*
Prentice Hall Hispanoamericana, S.A., *Mexico*
Prentice Hall of India Private Limited, *New Delhi*
Prentice Hall of Japan, Inc., *Tokyo*
Simon & Schuster Asia Pte. Ltd., *Singapore*
Editora Prentice Hall do Brasil, Ltda., *Rio de Janeiro*